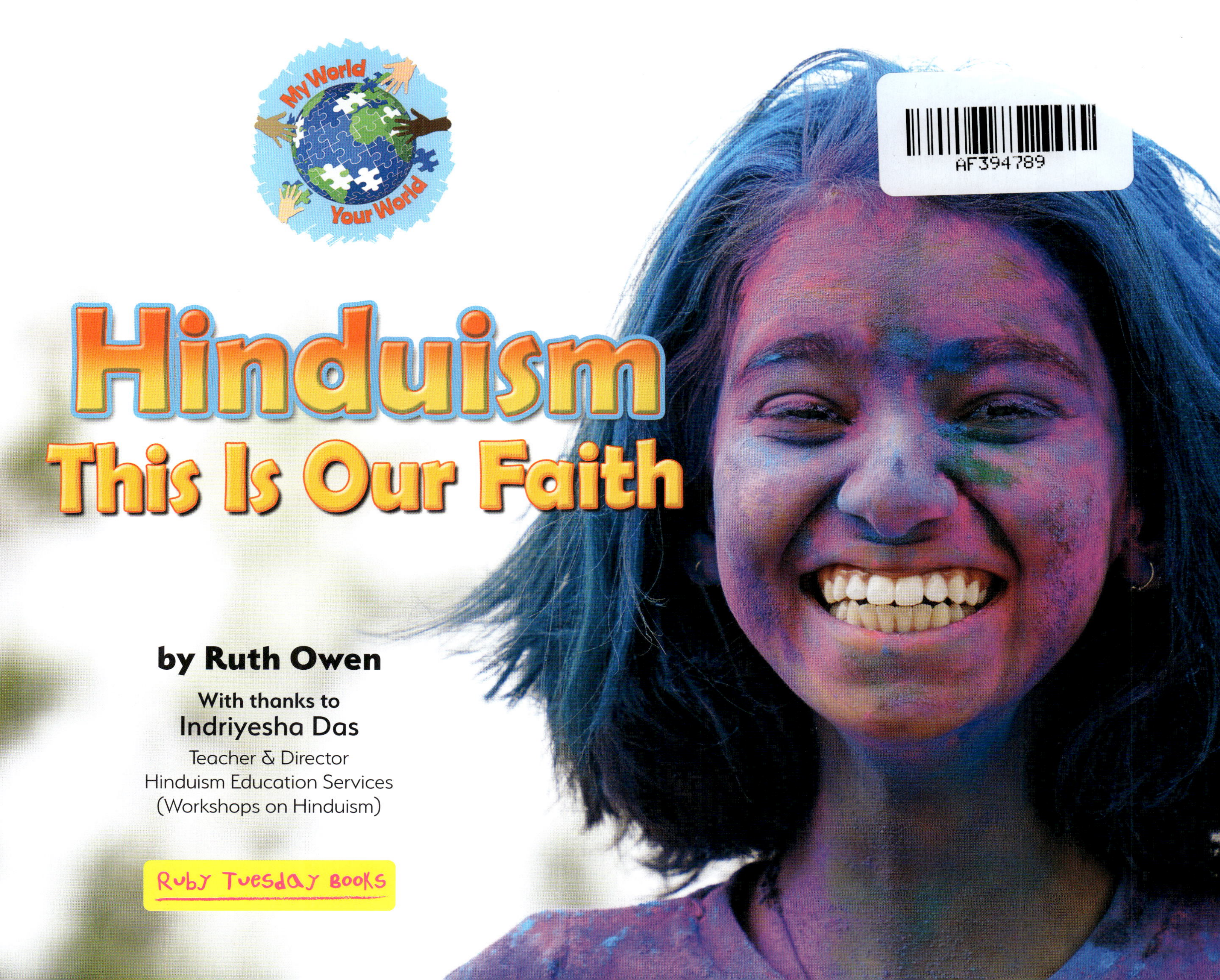

Hinduism
This Is Our Faith

by **Ruth Owen**

With thanks to
Indriyesha Das
Teacher & Director
Hinduism Education Services
(Workshops on Hinduism)

Ruby Tuesday Books

Published in 2026 by Ruby Tuesday Books Ltd.
Copyright © 2026 Ruby Tuesday Books Ltd.

Editor: Mark J. Sachner
Design & Production: Tammy West

Photo Credits:
Alamy: Cover (Rafayat Khan), 9 (Ira Berger), 11 (Ira Berger), 12B (Art Directors & TRIP), 14L (Jim West), 15 (ZUMA Press Inc), 19B (Amit Sardar), 21R (Sumanto Biswas); Shutterstock: 1 (Govind Jangir), 3B (Priti sinha), 4 (StockImageFactory.com), 5 (Monkey Business Images), 6L (Russamee), 6C (d odin), 6R (R. M. Nunes), 7TL (SB Creations), 7TR (Image Bug), 7B (Bappa Pabitra), 8L (Gopika S Nair), 8R (I Wei Huang), 10 (Elakshi Creative Business), 10BL (StockImageFactory.com), 12TL (Westock Productions), 13TL (Elakshi Creative Business), 13TR & 13B (StockImageFactory.com), 14R (SewCreamStudio), 16 (Ramniklal Modi), 17T (Bimal Bag), 17B (Rupendra Singh Rawat), 18L (Jayakumar), 18R (ashok India), 19T (V Drone), 20 (Dinesh Hukmani), 21 (Sumit Saraswat), 22 (V Drone), 23 (Raushan films), 23BC (Indian Food Images).

British Library Cataloguing in Publication Data (CIP) is available for this title.

ISBN 978-1-78856-210-2

Printed in Malta by Gutenberg Press

www.rubytuesdaybooks.com

Contents

Words shown in bold in the text are explained in the glossary.

Ganesha

This Is Our Faith

Hinduism is a faith that began in India thousands of years ago.

The people who follow this religious way of life are called Hindus.

Hindus believe that God lives in three places – everywhere, inside our hearts and far away in **heaven**.

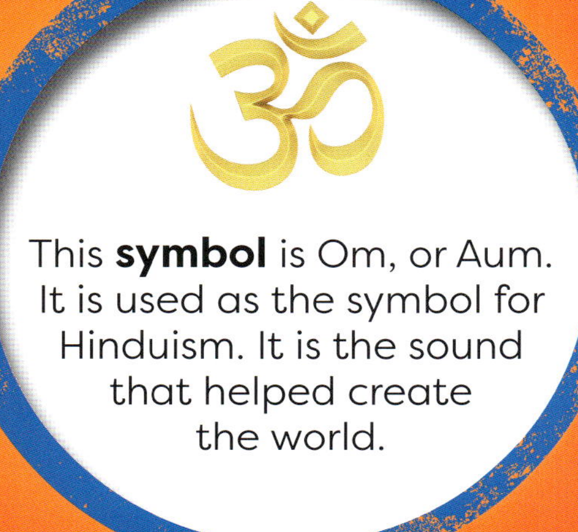

This **symbol** is Om, or Aum. It is used as the symbol for Hinduism. It is the sound that helped create the world.

Many Hindus now live outside of India, including in the UK.

God's energy which is everywhere is called
Brahman, **eternal spirit.**

Hindu Gods and Goddesses

Each Hindu god or goddess is a form of God, or one of God's helpers. The three most important gods are Brahma, Vishnu and Shiva.

Brahma is the creator of the Universe.

Vishnu takes care of the universe. He comes to Earth to help us. Vishnu takes different forms and names, such as Krishna.

Shiva is the destroyer of evil within the universe.

Sarasvati is the goddess of art, music and learning.

Lakshmi is the goddess of fortune who gives us wealth.

Welcome to a Mandir

A Hindu temple is called a mandir. Hindus worship in their local mandir.

Sacred statues of the gods and goddesses that are popular in that community live in the mandir.

Worshippers offer food to the gods, including fruit, sweets, rice and other cooked dishes.

After the food is **blessed** by the **priest**, it is called prasadam. The priest shares it with the worshippers.

"During worship, incense sticks are burned. The sweet-smelling smoke fills the room and reminds people of heaven."

The Ceremony of Arti

During puja, Hindus perform a **ceremony** called Arti, which welcomes God.

A burning lamp, incense and flowers are waved before the sacred statues or pictures of the gods and goddesses.

During Arti, worshippers sing hymns, ring bells and play musical instruments.

The lamp is an offering which shows our love to God. Everyone carefully passes their fingers over the flame.

Arti lamp
Plate

Then, to show respect to God, we touch our fingers to our foreheads. Next, we place money on the plate as an offering.

Our Daily Worship

Many Hindus worship every day at a shrine in their home.

The worshippers sing, pray, chant **mantras** and perform Arti.

Hindus have many holy books. The Vedas and the Bhagavad Gita are the most famous. Inside are stories, hymns and prayers. There is also advice on how to live a good life.

Pictures or statues of a family's favourite gods and goddesses stand on the shrine.

A shrine in a home in London.

Offerings of flowers, fruits, sweets, rice, water, milk, honey and money are placed at the shrine.

Living a Life of Kindness

For Hindus, being kind is very important.

They help others by giving money to charities and by helping to feed the hungry.

This is called Dana.

A box of toys for a charity to sell.

Hindus also help and serve others without wanting anything in return.

This is called Seva.

These young people in the USA are spending their free time cooking meals for homeless people.

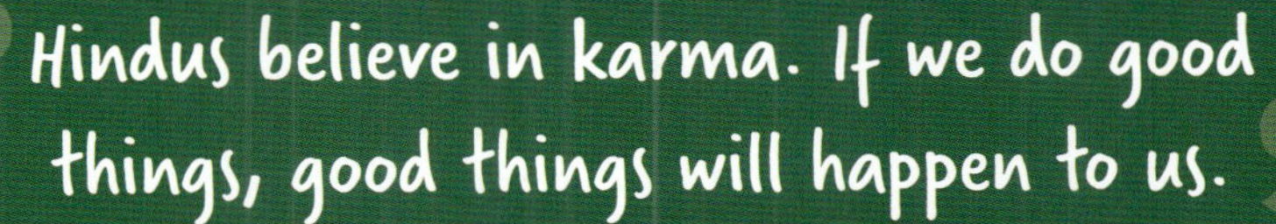

For Hindus, cows are especially holy.

15

New Baby Celebrations

A new baby's naming day is a time for prayer and celebration.

The father whispers the name into his baby's ear. Then the name is announced to everyone.

The family celebrates with music and a special meal.

A six-day-old baby

When a baby is about six months old, the family celebrates Annaprashana.

At this ceremony, the baby eats their first solid food of grains.

During Annaprashana, friends and family pray for the baby's health and happiness. Then the baby is fed their first grains, usually sweet rice pudding.

Welcome to a Hindu Wedding

A Hindu wedding is a sacred ceremony.

The bride and groom promise to stay together for life.

The bride's hands and feet are decorated with patterns made from henna.

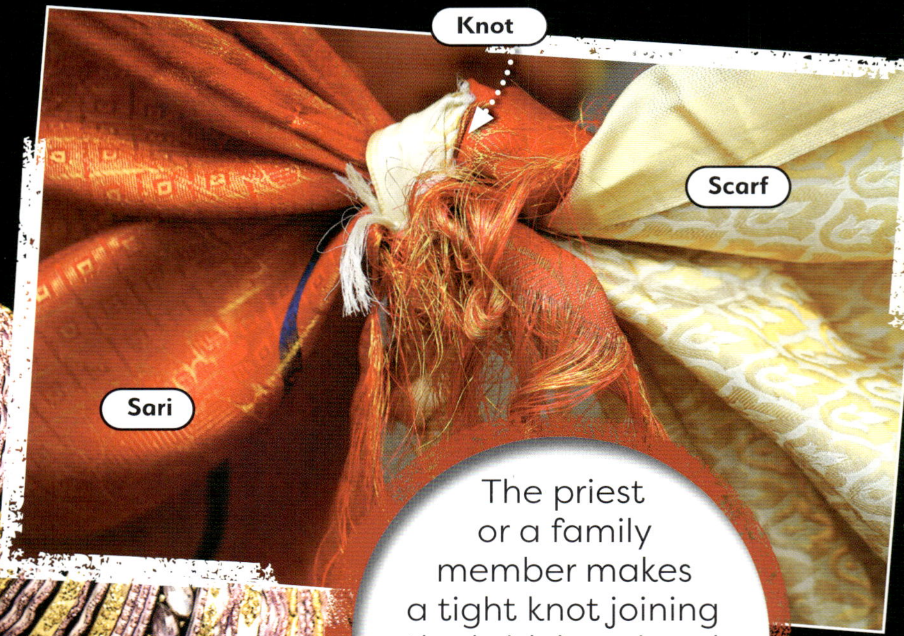

The priest or a family member makes a tight knot joining the bride's sari and the groom's scarf. This shows that they are now a couple.

Many Hindu brides wear a red sari. Red is a sacred and lucky colour. It's a symbol of energy, love and a strong marriage. It gives blessings for wealth and children.

Prayers and offerings are made to the god Ganesha.

The couple throw offerings of rice into the sacred fire.

The groom puts red powder on the bride's hair to show she is now a married woman.

Let's Celebrate! Holi

Holi is the Hindu festival of colours.

On the first day of Holi, people throw offerings of grains, seeds and decorated coconuts into bonfires.

At Holi, bonfires celebrate the victory of good over evil.

An evil witch named Holika tried to burn a religious little boy called Prahlada. But Vishnu protected Prahlada and burned Holika!

Holi lasts for two days in February or March.
This fun festival celebrates the arrival of spring.

On the second day of Holi, everyone gathers in the streets.

They throw coloured powdered paint over each other.

The god Krishna lived in a village in India over 5000 years ago. He looked after the cows and calves.

As a youth, Krishna and the milkmaids would play by throwing coloured powder and water over each other. What fun!

Let's Celebrate! Diwali

Diwali is the festival of lights. It celebrates the victory of light over darkness and of good over evil.

Diwali is the beginning of the Hindu new year.

People enjoy fireworks and decorate their homes with small oil lamps called divas.

Children in India acting in a play about Rama and Sita.

We tell stories of brave, good Prince Rama and his wife Sita. Rama and his friends went on a long journey to rescue Sita from an evil demon king.

At Diwali, Hindus visit friends and family and exchange gifts of sweets.

GLOSSARY

blessed
To be given and to receive God's protection and love.

ceremony
An occasion or event where people gather and particular actions are carried out – for example, a wedding ceremony.

eternal
Lasting forever.

heaven
In Hindu beliefs, heaven is God's home. There are also beautiful planets in this universe called the heavenly planets.

mantra
Important and powerful words or sounds that a person might repeat many times. Mantras can help a person feel calm, happy and closer to God.

priest
A religious leader.

prosperous
Successful in making or having money.

puja
Hindu worship. Puja can happen in a person's home or in a mandir.

sacred
Something that is special or holy. It is usually important because it is connected to God.

soul
In Hindu beliefs, the spiritual part of a living thing that goes on forever.

spirit
In Hindu beliefs, something that people cannot see, touch, hear, smell or taste, but which is real and without end.

symbol
An item, picture, sign, word or sound that stands for something else – for example, Om is the symbol of God or Brahman.

INDEX